*A LifeGuide®* **Bible Study**

PAUL

His Life and Teaching

10 STUDIES FOR INDIVIDUALS OR GROUPS

Jack Kuhatschek

With Notes for Leaders

IVP Connect

An imprint of InterVarsity Press
Downers Grove, Illinois

InterVarsity Press
P.O. Box 1400, Downers Grove, IL 60515-1426
World Wide Web: www.ivpress.com
E-mail: email@ivpress.com

InterVarsity Press® is the book-publishing division of InterVarsity Christian Fellowship/USA®,
a movement of students and faculty active on campus at hundreds of universities, colleges and
schools of nursing in the United States of America, and a member movement of the International
Fellowship of Evangelical Students. For information about local and regional activities, write Public
Relations Dept., InterVarsity Christian Fellowship/USA, 6400 Schroeder Rd., P.O. Box 7895,
Madison, WI 53707-7895, or visit the IVCF website at <www.intervarsity.org>.

LifeGuide® is a registered trademark of InterVarsity Christian Fellowship.

All Scripture quotations, unless otherwise indicated, are taken from the Holy Bible, New
International Version®. NIV®. Copyright ©1973, 1978, 1984 by International Bible Society.
Used by permission of Zondervan Publishing House. All rights reserved.

Study 3 is adapted from Self-Esteem, Jack Kuhatschek, revised edition, ©2002.

Study 7 is adapted from God's Comfort, Jack Kuhatschek, ©2004.

Cover image: zennie/iStockphoto

ISBN 978-0-8308-3139-5

Printed in the United States of America ∞

P 20 19 18 17 16 15 14 13 12 11 10 9 8 7 6 5 4 3

Y 27 26 25 24 23 22 21 20 19 18 17 16 15 14 13 12

Contents

Getting the Most Out of *Paul*

The first written description of the apostle Paul comes from a second-century document titled the *Acts of Paul and Thecla*.

> At length they saw a man coming (namely Paul), of a small stature with meeting eyebrows, bald head, bow-legged, strongly built, hollow-eyed, with a large crooked nose; he was full of grace, for sometimes he appeared as a man, sometimes he had the countenance of an angel.

Although many dispute the authenticity of this description, there are several references to Paul in the New Testament that help us to understand how others perceived him. For example, some of the Corinthians claimed, "His letters are weighty and forceful, but in person he is unimpressive and his speaking amounts to nothing" (2 Corinthians 10:10). These same people also said that Paul was "'timid' when face to face . . . but 'bold' when away!" (2 Corinthians 10:1). Paul admitted that he was not a "trained speaker" in the manner of first-century orators (2 Corinthians 11:6). And even though we don't know the exact nature of Paul's "thorn" (2 Corinthians 12), it clearly humbled him and made him feel weak.

Yet apart from Jesus himself, no one in the New Testament comes close to Paul's love for the Lord, his passion and dedication to the church, or his willingness to endure prolonged suffering for the sake of the gospel. In one of his letters to the church at Corinth, which questioned the validity of Paul's apostleship, he reluctantly defends himself by giving a summary of his accomplishments for Christ:

> What anyone else dares to boast about—I am speaking as a fool—I also dare to boast about. Are they Hebrews? So am I. Are they Israelites? So am I. Are they Abraham's descendants? So am I. Are they servants of Christ? (I am out of my mind to talk

like this.) I am more. I have worked much harder, been in prison more frequently, been flogged more severely, and been exposed to death again and again. Five times I received from the Jews the forty lashes minus one. Three times I was beaten with rods, once I was stoned, three times I was shipwrecked, I spent a night and a day in the open sea, I have been constantly on the move. I have been in danger from rivers, in danger from bandits, in danger from my own countrymen, in danger from Gentiles; in danger in the city, in danger in the country, in danger at sea; and in danger from false brothers. I have labored and toiled and have often gone without sleep; I have known hunger and thirst and have often gone without food; I have been cold and naked. Besides everything else, I face daily the pressure of my concern for all the churches. Who is weak, and I do not feel weak? Who is led into sin, and I do not inwardly burn? (2 Corinthians 11:21-29)

This LifeGuide will introduce you to one of the most fascinating people who ever lived in the service of Jesus Christ. We'll follow Paul's life and teachings from the moment of his conversion on the road to Damascus to his imprisonment in Rome at the end of the book of Acts—with brief stops along the way to dip into his letters to the churches. What we'll discover is a person who provides a superb example of what it means to experience the Lord's promise that "whoever loses his life for me and for the gospel will save it" (Mark 8:35).

Suggestions for Individual Study

1. As you begin each study, pray that God will speak to you through his Word.

2. Read the introduction to the study and respond to the personal reflection question or exercise. This is designed to help you focus on God and on the theme of the study.

3. Each study deals with a particular passage so that you can delve into the author's meaning in that context. Read and reread the passage to be studied. The questions are written using the language of the New International Version, so you may wish to use that version of the Bible. The New Revised Standard Version is also recommended.

4. This is an inductive Bible study, designed to help you discover for yourself what Scripture is saying. The study includes three types of questions. *Observation* questions ask about the basic facts: who, what, when, where and how. *Interpretation* questions delve into the meaning of the passage. *Application* questions help you discover the implications of the text for growing in Christ. These three keys unlock the treasures of Scripture.

Write your answers to the questions in the spaces provided or in a personal journal. Writing can bring clarity and deeper understanding of yourself and of God's Word.

5. It might be good to have a Bible dictionary handy. Use it to look up any unfamiliar words, names or places.

6. Use the prayer suggestion to guide you in thanking God for what you have learned and to pray about the applications that have come to mind.

7. You may want to go on to the suggestion under "Now or Later," or you may want to use that idea for your next study.

Suggestions for Members of a Group Study

1. Come to the study prepared. Follow the suggestions for individual study mentioned above. You will find that careful preparation will greatly enrich your time spent in group discussion.

2. Be willing to participate in the discussion. The leader of your group will not be lecturing. Instead, he or she will be encouraging the members of the group to discuss what they have learned. The leader will be asking the questions that are found in this guide.

3. Stick to the topic being discussed. Your answers should be based on the verses which are the focus of the discussion and not on outside authorities such as commentaries or speakers. These studies focus on a particular passage of Scripture. Only rarely should you refer to other portions of the Bible. This allows for everyone to participate in in-depth study on equal ground.

4. Be sensitive to the other members of the group. Listen attentively when they describe what they have learned. You may be surprised by their insights! Each question assumes a variety of answers. Many questions do not have "right" answers, particularly questions that aim at meaning or application. Instead the questions push us to explore the passage more thoroughly.

When possible, link what you say to the comments of others. Also, be affirming whenever you can. This will encourage some of the more hesitant members of the group to participate.

5. Be careful not to dominate the discussion. We are sometimes so eager to express our thoughts that we leave too little opportunity for others to respond. By all means participate! But allow others to also.

6. Expect God to teach you through the passage being discussed and through the other members of the group. Pray that you will have an enjoyable and profitable time together, but also that as a result of the study you will find ways that you can take action individually and/or as a group.

7. Remember that anything said in the group is considered confidential and should not be discussed outside the group unless specific permission is given to do so.

8. If you are the group leader, you will find additional suggestions at the back of the guide.

1

Blinded by the Light

Acts 9:1-31

Jane Austen's most famous novel, *Pride and Prejudice,* was originally titled *First Impressions.* Throughout the story readers discover that many first impressions later prove to be misguided: In a fit of anger, Elizabeth Bennet tells Mr. Darcy, "From the first moment I met you, your arrogance and conceit made me realize that you were the last man in the world that I could ever marry." And yet she later falls deeply in love with him and becomes his wife. Mr. Darcy himself is no better with first impressions. When his closest friend urges him to dance with Elizabeth, describing her as "very pretty," Darcy responds coldly, "She is tolerable; but not handsome enough to tempt *me.*" Yet later he completely reverses himself, declaring, "For it is many months since I have considered her as one of the handsomest women of my acquaintance."

GROUP DISCUSSION. Do you believe you should trust your first impressions of a person? Why or why not?

PERSONAL REFLECTION. When have you been mistaken in your first impression of someone?

The story of Saul's conversion is filled with irony and demonstrates how wrong our initial impressions can be—and how much a person can change. *Read Acts 9:1-31.*

1. How many times in this passage are people's thoughts about someone dramatically reversed?

2. In what ways would Saul's strong convictions have been challenged when he heard the answer to his question, "Who are you, Lord?" (vv. 1-5).

3. What do we learn about Jesus and his followers from the Lord's statement, "Why do you persecute me?" (v. 4).

4. Saul's blindness was real but also symbolic. What do you think he learned about himself and the Lord during his period of blindness (vv. 6-19)?

How was your life different before and after meeting the Lord?

5. In what ways does Ananias experience his own dramatic reversal (vv. 10-17)?

---

6. While it's easy to grasp how Saul could now preach that Jesus is the Son of God, how do you think he is able to "prove" to the Jews in Damascus that Jesus is the Messiah—especially since that contradicted everything he previously believed (vv. 20-22)?

---

7. The claim is often made today that reason and logical arguments are useless in bringing someone to faith in Christ. How would you respond to that claim, and why?

---

8. In Western culture today, theological disputes rarely result in violence. Why do you think the Jews of Paul's day—including Saul himself—were prone to violence toward those who believed in Jesus (vv. 22-25)?

---

9. In what ways does Saul's experience in Jerusalem mirror his life in Damascus after his conversion (vv. 26-31)?

10. Saul's conversion immediately led him to talk about Jesus with those around him who did not believe. To what extent do you follow his example, and why?

How can you become more vocal about your beliefs in Jesus and the good news?

Ask God to give spiritual sight to those around you who are blind to the truth about Jesus.

Now or Later

Spend some time thinking and perhaps journaling about the following question: In what ways have your beliefs about Jesus and the Christian faith changed since you first came to faith in Christ?

2

Proclaiming God's Promises

Acts 13:13-52

New discoveries are sometimes suppressed rather than embraced by those in authority. For example, in the early 1920s conventional scientific wisdom said that the sun was composed primarily of molten iron. But a young Harvard graduate student named Cecilia Payne disagreed. Her study of stellar spectra convinced her that hydrogen was the most abundant element in the sun and the other stars. When Henry Norris Russell, who was the leading authority on stellar spectra, saw her doctoral dissertation, he proclaimed that her conclusions were "impossible." The director of Harvard's Observatory, Harlow Shapley, pressured Payne to write that in spite of the data in her thesis, her results were "almost certainly not real." Yet four years later, Russell wrote his own paper in which he announced that the sun is made mostly of hydrogen. And in a strange twist of irony, Cecilia Payne received the prestigious Henry Norris Russell Prize in 1977 from the American Astronomical Society.

GROUP DISCUSSION. Why do you think people often suppress the truth rather than embrace it?

PERSONAL REFLECTION. When are you tempted to rationalize or deny truths about yourself?

In Acts 13 Paul preaches the good news to his fellow Jews in Antioch. But their response is the opposite of what Paul desires. *Read Acts 13:13-52.*

1. As the Jewish people spread throughout the world, so did their places of worship and instruction known as synagogues. How does the synagogue in Antioch provide a natural setting for Paul to preach the gospel (vv. 14-15)?

2. Why do you think Paul begins his message by giving a brief history of Israel (vv. 16-23)?

3. What arguments does Paul use to demonstrate that Jesus is the fulfillment of God's promises to the Jewish people (vv. 23-37)?

Do you think these types of arguments are effective with people today? Why or why not?

4. Paul's statements in verses 38-39 form the heart of what he later writes to those living in Galatia—the region of Asia Minor surrounding and including Antioch. What is the essence of this proclamation?

5. What evidence is there that both Jews and Gentiles initially responded in a positive way to Paul's message (vv. 42-44)?

Why do you think there was such widespread interest in what Paul was saying?

6. Luke, who is the author of the book of Acts, tells us, "When the Jews saw the crowds, they were filled with jealousy and talked abusively against what Paul was saying" (v. 45). What may have formed the basis of their jealousy and hostility?

7. What are some of the reasons people today are hostile toward the gospel?

8. Many Jews in Paul's day had forgotten their God-given mission (Acts 13:47; Isaiah 49:6). How can we avoid being self-absorbed today and keep our focus on being a light to others?

9. In first-century Judaism, Gentiles were considered outcasts. Who would fit that description in our society?

How can we make a special effort to reach out to those people?

10. Why do you think those rejected by others are most joyful when embraced by Jesus and the church (vv. 48, 52)?

Pray that God will give you compassion for those who are considered outcasts in our society.

Now or Later

Take time this week to reach out to someone who others consider an outcast. How can you show the love of Christ to that person in practical ways?

3

Poor Yet Rich

1 Corinthians 4:8-13; 2 Corinthians 6:3-10

A few years ago a mission agency was looking for recruits. They ran an ad showing a missionary fording a river in a poor section of Africa. The man was struggling under the weight of a heavy backpack in the heat of the sun. The caption under the ad read: "In high school, John was voted the man most likely to succeed. Now look at him." Clearly John had a different idea of success.

We all know that the world's standards of success are not the same as God's. Yet we often assume that God owes us a comfortable home, a secure job, decent clothes and a minimum of turmoil. When one or more of these "rights" eludes us, our faith can begin to plummet.

GROUP DISCUSSION. When hardships or difficulties enter your life, do you ever feel that God has abandoned you? Why or why not?

PERSONAL REFLECTION. How do you relate to God when you are in the midst of personal difficulties?

In these two passages in Corinthians, Paul tells us we need to re-adjust our thinking and our expectations about success. *Read 1 Corinthians 4:8-13.*

1. How would you describe Paul's mood or tone in these verses?

---

2. Based on Paul's description in chapter 4, verses 8 and 10, how do you think the Corinthians viewed themselves?

---

3. We normally view wealth, wisdom, honor and strength as desirable. Why then do you think Paul scolds the Corinthians?

---

4. How does Paul portray the life of an apostle (4:9-13)?

---

5. How do you think you would you feel toward God if he allowed you to be homeless, hungry and thirsty, ill-clad, and brutally treated?

Read 2 Corinthians 6:3-10.

---

6. What details do these verses add to our portrait of Paul's hardships?

What do they reveal about his character?

---

7. In spite of his poverty and hardships, how do you think Paul is able to maintain a healthy view of God and himself (6:8-10)?

---

8. The Bible tells us that suffering precedes glory (2 Corinthians 4:17). In what ways are you tempted to skip over the first part, seeking glory in this present age? Explain.

---

9. How do your personal goals and expectations need to be revised in light of this study?

10. How can you have a sense of dignity and joy, regardless of your present circumstances?

Thank God for the hope we have in Christ. Ask him to help you readjust your thinking about life during this present age.

Now or Later

In Mark 8:34-35 Jesus said, "If anyone would come after me, he must deny himself and take up his cross and follow me. For whoever wants to save his life will lose it, but whoever loses his life for me and for the gospel will save it." How do his words challenge your view of life now and in the future?

4

The Power of Praise

During the spring of 1738 the great Methodist hymn writer Charles Wesley became severely ill. During this time he read Martin Luther's commentary on Galatians and spent time with a godly Moravian named Peter Böhler; Wesley gave his life to Christ on May 21. He wrote in his journal: "At midnight I gave myself up to Christ: assured I was safe, sleeping or waking. I had continued experience of his power to overcome all temptation; and confessed, with joy and surprise, that he was able to do exceedingly abundantly for me, above what I can ask or think." Two days later he wrote the hymn "And Can It Be That I Should Gain?" which was inspired by the story of Paul and the Philippian jailer in Acts 16:16-40.

GROUP DISCUSSION. How has your worship been enhanced by classic hymns or contemporary Christian music?

PERSONAL REFLECTION. What types of events in your life are most likely to evoke praise to God?

The story of the Philippian jailer in Acts 16 has been a favorite of Christians for centuries because it demonstrates the power of praise and the liberating effects of the gospel. *Read Acts 16:16-40.*

1. Imagine that you are an eyewitness to the events in this passage. What parts would you highlight in telling the story to friends and family?

2. Even though the slave girl announces the truth about Paul and his companions, why do you think Paul becomes so troubled by her behavior (vv. 16-18)?

3. How does the situation escalate after the owners of the slave girl realize their hope of making money is gone (vv. 19-24)?

4. A prison seems an odd place to pray and sing hymns to God (v. 25). Why do you think Paul and Silas are able to praise God in these circumstances?

5. Describe a situation in your life where you were able to praise God in the midst of suffering or hardship.

6. What are the immediate effects of the earthquake and its "aftershocks" throughout the night (vv. 26-34)?

---

7. Why do you think Charles Wesley viewed the events of verses 26-30 as a beautiful illustration of what happens during conversion?

---

8. Paul decides to confront the magistrates instead of leaving the city quietly (vv. 35-37). What do you suppose he hopes to accomplish?

In what ways do his efforts succeed (vv. 38-40)?

---

9. Like Paul, we are called to proclaim the gospel. What does this passage reveal about both the joys and the difficulties we might encounter?

10. What difficulties and joys have you experienced when you've shared the gospel with others?

Spend some time praising God for your own release from spiritual prison and the chains that bound you before you were saved by Jesus Christ.

Now or Later

Take time this week to be alone with God with only your Bible and a hymnal or a CD that contains worship music. Devote yourself to prayer and praise.

5

Becoming a
Spiritual Mentor

Acts 20:13-38

Throughout much of my life, Billy Graham has been the elder states-
man of evangelicalism and a godly example to the world. During the
1960s he refused to preach to segregated audiences and tore down a
rope that crusade organizers had used to divide the audience. He remained faithful to his wife, Ruth, while many other evangelists were
exposed for immorality. He has demonstrated financial integrity, always taking a fixed salary, while many television preachers fleeced
their viewers. And although he has been a friend and adviser to several presidents, he has avoided entanglements in politics, focusing
instead on his calling to preach the gospel throughout the earth. According to the Billy Graham Evangelistic Association, he has preached
to live audiences of 215 million people in 185 countries and territo-
ries. And his televised audiences reached into the billions.

GROUP DISCUSSION. What Christians have you known who have been
godly examples or even mentors?

PERSONAL REFLECTION. Why do you think it's important to have godly
role models in your life?

Paul didn't just preach the gospel, he lived it and was a godly example to others. *Read Acts 20:13-38.*

1. When the elders arrive from Ephesus, Paul reminds them of how he both lived and taught during his time with them (vv. 17-35). What does he emphasize about his lifestyle?

2. What is the focus of his preaching and teaching?

3. Why do you think Paul feels it's necessary to describe the hardships that await him, as well as his inner resolve (vv. 22-24)?

Based on these three verses, what do you learn about Paul's values?

4. What are the primary values that motivate you in life?

How are these values evident in your lifestyle?

---

5. According to Paul, what does it mean to be good shepherds of the church of God (vv. 25-31)?

---

6. Some people claim today that how we live is far more important than what we believe. How do you think Paul would respond to this claim?

---

7. The expression "wolf in sheep's clothing" might have come from verses 25-31. How can we discern whether there is a wolf among God's sheep?

---

8. In spite of Paul's severe warnings, what gives him confidence that the church in Ephesus will survive (v. 32)?

9. Again, how is the purity of Paul's motives evident in his lifestyle (vv. 33-35)?

10. Why is our attitude toward money often a strong indicator of our spiritual maturity?

11. Paul's farewell to the Ephesian elders concludes with prayer, tears and affection. What does this scene reveal about Christian relationships?

Pray that the Lord will enable you to be a godly example to others through the consistency of your beliefs and actions.

Now or Later

Take time to reflect on how your beliefs, passions and lifestyle compare to what you observe about Paul in this passage. What adjustments do you need to make in light of your reflections? What practices can help you make those adjustments?

6

Truth on Trial

Acts 25:23–26:32

We normally think of an apology as synonymous with saying "I'm sorry." But in classical Greek the word *apologia* meant making a formal speech to reply to and rebut legal charges. Plato referred to Socrates's defense to the jurors in Athens as "The Apology of Socrates." Later Christian apologists, such as Tertullian and Justin Martyr, presented carefully reasoned defenses of the faith to secular readers. When the apostle Paul makes his "defense" to Festus and Agrippa in Acts 26:2, he uses the word *apologia*. But in his case, it is not only Paul himself but the very truth of the gospel that is on trial.

GROUP DISCUSSION. How would you explain the difference between defending yourself and being defensive?

PERSONAL REFLECTION. When you have done something wrong and someone confronts you about it, are you more likely to defend yourself or to say you're sorry?

As the scene opens in this passage, Paul is brought before Herod Agrippa II, the great-grandson of Herod the Great. Agrippa is accompanied by his sister, Bernice, who was often at his side, and by Festus, the governor. *Read Acts 25:23–26:32.*

1. What light does Festus shed on Paul's case in 25:23-27 (see also 25:13-22)?

2. Paul's speech follows the pattern of first-century legal defenses, beginning with his introductory address to the king (26:2-3). How does Paul feel about this opportunity?

3. The second part of Paul's legal defense is the narration of events (26:4-18). How does Paul establish that his lifestyle and beliefs are consistent with Judaism, which was a legal religion in the Roman Empire (26:4-8)?

4. Why do you think Paul feels it is important to describe his initial opposition to Jesus and his followers (26:9-11)?

5. What new details of Paul's conversion do we learn from his own retelling of it here in Acts 26 (see Acts 9 for comparison)?

6. Paul's defense to Agrippa is what we might today call a "testimony." When have you had opportunities to tell the story of your conversion?

What do you try to emphasize when telling your story?

7. The third and final part of Paul's legal defense is the "proof" of his case (26:19-23). How does Paul sum up his argument?

8. Obviously, Paul's carefully constructed speech fails to convince Agrippa (26:24, 28). Why are logic, argumentation and even testimony not enough to bring people to Christ?

What else is needed?

9. How is Paul's passion for the gospel and for those who hear it evident in his exchange with Agrippa in 26:25-29?

Does your life demonstrate a similar passion? Why or why not?

10. Ironically, Paul might have been set free at this point if he had not previously appealed to Caesar (see Acts 25:11-12). How is God's sovereignty seen in this situation?

Pray that God will enable you to "be prepared to give an answer to everyone who asks you to give the reason for the hope that you have" in Christ (1 Peter 3:15).

Now or Later

To what extent do you feel prepared to tell the story of your coming to faith in Christ? What might you do to become better prepared for future conversations? This week consider writing out a brief summary of your conversion story. Be prepared to read it to the members of your group at the next meeting.

7

Strength in Weakness

In recent years superheroes have become a fascination for both Hollywood and moviegoers. We've been treated to Spider-Man, the X-Men, Batman, Iron Man and the Fantastic Four. There has also been the Watchmen, Superman, Catwoman, Elektra, Ghost Rider and the incredible Hulk.

In a sense, these superheroes have become icons of our culture. We long to rise above ordinary humanity to achieve the status of demigods who are stronger, faster, smarter and more powerful than our peers.

GROUP DISCUSSION. In what ways does society reward personal beauty, power, size and strength? How does that make you feel?

PERSONAL REFLECTION. What one weakness of yours have you often wished you could turn into a strength?

God's Word stands in sharp contrast to our culture: "'Not by might nor by power, but by my Spirit,' says the LORD Almighty" (Zechariah 4:6). In 2 Corinthians 12 Paul discovers that God's power is best displayed in those who are humble and weak. *Read 2 Corinthians 12:1-10.*

1. Beginning in 11:16, Paul reluctantly began "boasting" to silence his opponents. What additional incident does he boast about in 12:1-4?

2. If this experience had happened to me, I would be tempted to write an entire book about it! Explain in your own words why Paul prefers to refrain from boasting and gives such sketchy details, avoiding even the use of his own name (vv. 1-6).

3. In what situation are you most tempted to boast about yourself? Why?

4. When Paul was tempted to float aloft with conceit, how did God nail his feet to earth (v. 7)?

Besides keeping him humble, what effects did Paul's "thorn" have on him?

5. Like Paul, we often assume that God's power is best displayed by him *removing* our weaknesses (v. 8). Why does the Lord sometimes refuse to remove our "thorns" (v. 9)?

How would you explain in your own words the meaning of God's reply to Paul and us?

6. Scholars have speculated in vain about the precise nature of Paul's thorn. Yet, according to Paul, what various types of difficulties might qualify as thorns (vv. 9-10)?

Why has Paul learned not only to endure such thorns but to "delight" in them?

7. What weakness, insult, hardship, persecution or difficulty feels like a thorn in your flesh?

8. If God chooses not to remove your thorn, how might it be a source of his grace and power in your life?

Thank God for his sufficient grace. Ask him to perfect his power in your weakness.

Now or Later

According to Paul, the Lord deliberately chose the foolish people of the world "to shame the wise." He chose the weak people of the world "to shame the strong." He chose the lowly people of this world and the despised people "to nullify the things that are" (1 Corinthians 1:27-28). Why do you think the Lord's long-range goal is to make the somebodies of this world into nobodies and the nobodies into some-bodies?

8

Feeling Safe
in a Storm

Acts 27:1-44

Samuel Kelly, an eighteenth-century seaman, wrote: "Seamen are neither reckoned among the living nor the dead, their whole lives being spent in jeopardy. No sooner is one peril over, but another comes rolling on, like the waves of a full-grown sea."

If Kelly's description was true in the eighteenth century, then imagine the peril of sailors in New Testament times. A typical merchant ship of the first century "reached almost 200 feet in length, had sails, and carried oars for emergencies. One large ship could transport several hundred passengers in addition to cargo."

GROUP DISCUSSION. Describe the worst storm you've ever seen and experienced, and how you felt during that storm.

PERSONAL REFLECTION. What makes you feel safe during the storms of life?

Life brings many storms. In this passage Paul is en route to Rome aboard a merchant ship when he and the crew are caught in a terrifying and life-threatening storm. *Read Acts 27:1-44.*

1. What details in this passage give evidence of an eyewitness account?

2. How do verses 1-13 set the stage for the drama that follows?

3. In what ways do the sailors struggle in vain against the power of the storm (vv. 14-20)?

4. When have you felt helpless and hopeless in the midst of a personal storm?

5. Why is Paul able to encourage those on board the ship in a seemingly hopeless situation (vv. 21-26)?

6. If God was determined to bring Paul safely to Rome to proclaim the gospel, then why didn't he simply provide smooth sailing throughout the journey?

7. Paul has already assured those on board by what God had told him: "God has graciously given you the lives of all who sail with you" (v. 24). Why then must he warn the centurion, "Unless these men stay with the ship, you cannot be saved" (v. 31)?

Some Christian traditions emphasize God's sovereignty, while others stress human responsibility. How does this passage show the importance of keeping both in proper balance?

8. If you had been one of the soldiers or sailors on board the ship, how would you have been encouraged by Paul's calm trust in God (vv. 33-38)?

9. In what ways can your faith be an encouragement to others during difficult times?

Ask God for the strength to trust him not only in good times but also during hardships.

Now or Later

Think of someone among your family or friends who is going through one of life's storms. Take time to pray for that person and, if possible, provide them with words of comfort and encouragement.

9

Finding Hope
in God's Kingdom

Acts 28:11-31

A story is told about a man who was convinced he was dead. His family and friends were so concerned about him that they sent him to a doctor in hopes of ending the man's confusion. After a futile discussion with the patient, the doctor decided to pursue a new argument—that dead men don't bleed. He pulled several medical volumes off of his shelves and gave them to the patient, asking him to read selected articles at home during the following week.

A few days later the man returned to the doctor's office carrying the borrowed books. "I've read every article you mentioned," said the man, "and I'm completely convinced that dead men don't bleed." At that point, seeing his opportunity, the doctor pricked the man's arm with a needle, and blood appeared immediately.

The man looked down at his bleeding arm with astonishment and proclaimed: "My God! Dead men *do* bleed!"

Some people are so convinced of their own opinions that no amount of argument or evidence will persuade them otherwise.

GROUP DISCUSSION. What experiences have you had lately in talking with neighbors or coworkers about Jesus and the gospel?

PERSONAL REFLECTION. To what extent did arguments and evidence have an impact on your becoming a Christian?

In this session we find that the apostle Paul finally arrives in Rome. Although he is received warmly by the Christian church, he has some difficulty with the Jewish community. *Read Acts 28:11-31.*

1. What seem to be Paul's attitude and primary concerns as he nears and then finally arrives in Rome?

2. Why do you think Paul's Roman guards seem to disappear into the background in verses 11-15?

3. Why do you suppose Paul was allowed to live in his own rented house rather than in a Roman prison (v. 16)?

4. How does Paul defend his innocence in verses 17-22?

Why do you think he believes this is so important in the current circumstances?

5. Some Christians today claim that sincere faith in God is sufficient for salvation, and therefore people do not need to explicitly believe in

Jesus Christ and the gospel to be saved. How do Paul's actions in verse 23—and throughout the book of Acts—run counter to that notion?

6. Some of the Jews believed Paul while others disagreed with him (vv. 24-25). What all does this reveal about the work of spreading the good news of Christ?

7. Paul quotes from Isaiah 6 in verses 26-27, mentioning the eyes, the ears and the heart. How does this prophecy reveal the nature of unbelief?

8. What is the difference between hearing God's words with our ears versus truly hearing him?

How should this be a warning to us as we study the Scriptures?

9. In verse 28 Paul explains once again the basis of his mission to the Gentiles. Why do you think this argument was important to those in the early church?

10. The focus of Paul's message in verses 30-31 and verse 23 is on both the kingdom of God and the Lord Jesus Christ. How are these two emphases interconnected?

How do they provide hope for people throughout the world?

11. The book of Acts concludes with a final statement about Paul's passionate evangelistic activity. What impact should his example have on us today?

Pray that your life will be a living testimony to the hope we have in Jesus Christ.

Now or Later

The stories in the book of Acts began in the first century, but church history is filled with many other stories of what God has done through men and women committed to him—people such as Augustine of Hippo, Martin Luther, John Wesley, Hudson Taylor, Charles Spurgeon and Amy Carmichael. Consider reading the biography of one of these people, who are part of God's never-ending story.

10

Experiencing Joy in Sufferings

Philippians 1:12-26

In 1883 a young Theodore Roosevelt decided to hunt buffalo in the Dakota Badlands. Teddy hired a guide named Joe Ferris, and the two set off on horseback. The first few days it rained constantly, and the riders returned to camp each evening covered from head to toe in thick, sticky mud. Finally, one day they spotted three buffalo in the distance. They got off their horses and "wriggled like snakes through the underbrush. Roosevelt blundered into a bed of cactus and filled his hands with spines."

When he later tried to get off a shot, Roosevelt's horse wheeled around and the rifle banged into his forehead, creating a nasty gash that caused blood to flow into his eyes. At one point the animal charged both men, and they narrowly escaped. Then the buffalo vanished into the darkness. They hadn't had any water for over nine hours, but when they found a puddle it was so slimy that it was like gelatin, and they could hardly stand more than a mouthful. They had a hard biscuit for dinner and then curled up in their blankets, using their saddles for pillows. Their horses were tied to their saddle horns, and about midnight they were rudely awakened as their saddles were yanked from beneath their heads as their horses sped off into the distance.

When they finally found the horses and returned to camp, it

started raining again, and before long they were lying in four inches of water. Author Edmund Morris writes: "Shivering between sodden blankets, Ferris heard Roosevelt muttering something. To Joe's complete disbelief, the dude was saying, 'By Godfrey, but this is fun!'"

GROUP DISCUSSION. How would you answer the question "What makes one person's misery another one's joy?"

PERSONAL REFLECTION. When have you felt joy during difficult circumstances, and why?

Throughout Paul's life he experienced extreme hardship, persecution and years in prison. Yet he somehow rose above those circumstances and expressed a joy that seems to defy explanation. *Read Philippians 1:12-26.*

1. What details do we learn about Paul's circumstances from this passage?

2. Paul is able to have joy in prison because he has a different set of values than most people. According to verses 12-18, what does he value even more than his personal freedom and comfort?

Why do you think he places such a high value on what's happening around him?

3. If someone were to closely observe your life over the past few months, what would they conclude about the value you place on sharing the gospel?

What steps might you take to follow the example of Paul and his supporters?

4. Paul speaks of Christ being "exalted in my body" (v. 20) and then makes the bold statement: "For to me, to live is Christ" (v. 21). What do you think he means?

5. Paul appears to value death even more than life (vv. 21-23). Assuming that he does not have a morbid death wish, why might he look forward to what most people fear?

6. How should knowing Christ transform our views of both life and death?

7. What evidence do you see in verses 24-26 that Paul values the welfare of others more than he does his personal well-being?

8. Although Paul does not mention the Great Commandments (Matthew 22:36-40) in this passage, how do his values clearly reflect them?

9. Paul was able to be joyful in sufferings because he valued (a) preaching the gospel more than his personal freedom or comfort, (b) death even more than life and (c) the welfare of others more than his own well-being. How might these same values enable you to be more joyful during difficult times?

Ask God to reshape your values so that you are able to find true joy in what pleases him.

Now or Later

Reflect on those things in life that give you the greatest joy and the deepest sorrow. What do they reveal about your values? How do your values compare with those of the apostle Paul?

Leader's Notes

MY GRACE IS SUFFICIENT FOR YOU. (2 COR 12:9)

Leading a Bible discussion can be an enjoyable and rewarding experience. But it can also be *scary*—especially if you've never done it before. If this is your feeling, you're in good company. When God asked Moses to lead the Israelites out of Egypt, he replied, "O Lord, please send someone else to do it!" (Ex 4:13). It was the same with Solomon, Jeremiah and Timothy, but God helped these people in spite of their weaknesses, and he will help you as well.

You don't need to be an expert on the Bible or a trained teacher to lead a Bible discussion. The idea behind these inductive studies is that the leader guides group members to discover for themselves what the Bible has to say. This method of learning will allow group members to remember much more of what is said than a lecture would.

These studies are designed to be led easily. As a matter of fact, the flow of questions through the passage from observation to interpretation to application is so natural that you may feel that the studies lead themselves. This study guide is also flexible. You can use it with a variety of groups—student, professional, neighborhood or church groups. Each study takes forty-five to sixty minutes in a group setting.

There are some important facts to know about group dynamics and encouraging discussion. The suggestions listed below should enable you to effectively and enjoyably fulfill your role as leader.

Preparing for the Study

1. Ask God to help you understand and apply the passage in your own life. Unless this happens, you will not be prepared to lead others. Pray too for the various members of the group. Ask God to open your hearts to the message of his Word and motivate you to action.

2. Read the introduction to the entire guide to get an overview of the entire book and the issues which will be explored.

3. As you begin each study, read and reread the assigned Bible passage to familiarize yourself with it.

4. This study guide is based on the New International Version of the Bible. It will help you and the group if you use this translation as the basis for your study and discussion.

5. Carefully work through each question in the study. Spend time in meditation and reflection as you consider how to respond.

6. Write your thoughts and responses in the space provided in the study guide. This will help you to express your understanding of the passage clearly.

7. It might help to have a Bible dictionary handy. Use it to look up any unfamiliar words, names or places. (For additional help on how to study a passage, see chapter five of *How to Lead a LifeGuide Bible Study,* InterVarsity Press.)

8. Consider how you can apply the Scripture to your life. Remember that the group will follow your lead in responding to the studies. They will not go any deeper than you do.

9. Once you have finished your own study of the passage, familiarize yourself with the leader's notes for the study you are leading. These are designed to help you in several ways. First, they tell you the purpose the study guide author had in mind when writing the study. Take time to think through how the study questions work together to accomplish that purpose. Second, the notes provide you with additional background information or suggestions on group dynamics for various questions. This information can be useful when people have difficulty understanding or answering a question. Third, the leader's notes can alert you to potential problems you may encounter during the study.

10. If you wish to remind yourself of anything mentioned in the leader's notes, make a note to yourself below that question in the study.

Leading the Study

1. Begin the study on time. Open with prayer, asking God to help the group to understand and apply the passage.

2. Be sure that everyone in your group has a study guide. Encourage the group to prepare beforehand for each discussion by reading the introduction to the guide and by working through the questions in the study.

3. At the beginning of your first time together, explain that these studies are meant to be discussions, not lectures. Encourage the members of the group to participate. However, do not put pressure on those who may be hesitant to speak during the first few sessions. You may want to suggest the following guidelines to your group.

☐ Stick to the topic being discussed.

☐ Your responses should be based on the verses which are the focus of the discussion and not on outside authorities such as commentaries or speakers.

□ These studies focus on a particular passage of Scripture. Only rarely should you refer to other portions of the Bible. This allows for everyone to participate in in-depth study on equal ground.

□ Anything said in the group is considered confidential and will not be discussed outside the group unless specific permission is given to do so.

□ We will listen attentively to each other and provide time for each person present to talk.

□ We will pray for each other.

4. Have a group member read the introduction at the beginning of the discussion.

5. Every session begins with a group discussion question. The question or activity is meant to be used before the passage is read. The question introduces the theme of the study and encourages group members to begin to open up. Encourage as many members as possible to participate, and be ready to get the discussion going with your own response.

This section is designed to reveal where our thoughts or feelings need to be transformed by Scripture. That is why it is especially important not to read the passage before the discussion question is asked. The passage will tend to color the honest reactions people would otherwise give because they are, of course, supposed to think the way the Bible does.

You may want to supplement the group discussion question with an icebreaker to help people to get comfortable. See the community section of *Small Group Idea Book* for more ideas.

You also might want to use the personal reflection question with your group. Either allow a time of silence for people to respond individually or discuss it together.

6. Have a group member (or members if the passage is long) read aloud the passage to be studied. Then give people several minutes to read the passage again silently so that they can take it all in.

7. Question 1 will generally be an overview question designed to briefly survey the passage. Encourage the group to look at the whole passage, but try to avoid getting sidetracked by questions or issues that will be addressed later in the study.

8. As you ask the questions, keep in mind that they are designed to be used just as they are written. You may simply read them aloud. Or you may prefer to express them in your own words.

There may be times when it is appropriate to deviate from the study guide. For example, a question may have already been answered. If so, move on to the next question. Or someone may raise an important question not covered in the guide. Take time to discuss it, but try to keep the group from going off on tangents.

9. Avoid answering your own questions. If necessary, repeat or rephrase

them until they are clearly understood. Or point out something you read in the leader's notes to clarify the context or meaning. An eager group quickly becomes passive and silent if they think the leader will do most of the talking.

10. Don't be afraid of silence. People may need time to think about the question before formulating their answers.

11. Don't be content with just one answer. Ask, "What do the rest of you think?" or "Anything else?" until several people have given answers to the question.

12. Acknowledge all contributions. Try to be affirming whenever possible. Never reject an answer. If it is clearly off-base, ask, "Which verse led you to that conclusion?" or again, "What do the rest of you think?"

13. Don't expect every answer to be addressed to you, even though this will probably happen at first. As group members become more at ease, they will begin to truly interact with each other. This is one sign of healthy discussion.

14. Don't be afraid of controversy. It can be very stimulating. If you don't resolve an issue completely, don't be frustrated. Move on and keep it in mind for later. A subsequent study may solve the problem.

15. Periodically summarize what the group has said about the passage. This helps to draw together the various ideas mentioned and gives continuity to the study. But don't preach.

16. At the end of the Bible discussion you may want to allow group members a time of quiet to work on an idea under "Now or Later." Then discuss what you experienced. Or you may want to encourage group members to work on these ideas between meetings. Give an opportunity during the session for people to talk about what they are learning.

17. Conclude your time together with conversational prayer, adapting the prayer suggestion at the end of the study to your group. Ask for God's help in following through on the commitments you've made.

18. End on time.

Many more suggestions and helps are found in *How to Lead a LifeGuide Bible Study.*

Components of Small Groups

A healthy small group should do more than study the Bible. There are four components to consider as you structure your time together.

Nurture. Small groups help us to grow in our knowledge and love of God. Bible study is the key to making this happen and is the foundation of your small group.

Community. Small groups are a great place to develop deep friendships with other Christians. Allow time for informal interaction before and after each study. Plan activities and games that will help you get to know each other. Spend time having fun together going on a picnic or cooking dinner together.

Worship and prayer. Your study will be enhanced by spending time praising God together in prayer or song. Pray for each other's needs and keep track of how God is answering prayer in your group. Ask God to help you to apply what you are learning in your study.

Outreach. Reaching out to others can be a practical way of applying what you are learning, and it will keep your group from becoming self-focused. Host a series of evangelistic discussions for your friends or neighbors. Clean up the yard of an elderly friend. Serve at a soup kitchen together, or spend a day working on a Habitat house.

Many more suggestions and helps in each of these areas are found in *Small Group Idea Book.* Information on building a small group can be found in *Small Group Leaders' Handbook* and *The Big Book on Small Groups* (both from InterVarsity Press). Reading through one of these books would be worth your time.

Study 1. Blinded by the Light. Acts 9:1-31.

Purpose: To understand how Saul, the murderer of Christians, became Paul, the great apostle of Jesus Christ.

Question 1. Your group should consider Paul himself, Ananias, those who heard Paul in Damascus, the disciples in Jerusalem and the apostles.

Question 2. Prior to his conversion, Saul obviously thought that Jesus was an imposter and the disciples were traitors to Judaism. He would not have believed in Jesus' resurrection, nor would he have believed he was the Messiah promised in the Old Testament. On the road to Damascus, Saul's world was turned upside down.

Question 3. Jesus tells Saul that by persecuting Christians, he is actually persecuting Jesus. That thought later became an important feature in Paul's theology of the church being the body of Christ (see 1 Cor 12:27 and Eph 1:22-23 for examples).

Question 6. Saul was a highly educated man who had studied under Rabbi Gamaliel (Acts 22:3). Saul knew the overarching story of the Old Testament as well as its details, but his understanding did not grasp the need for the Messiah to suffer and die for the sins of the people. After meeting Jesus on the road to Damascus, Saul would have been confronted with his error and would have reexamined the story in light of the reality of Jesus. See the story of the two disciples on the road to Emmaus (Lk 24:13-35) for a similar example.

Question 8. I mention Western culture because in reality theological disputes result in violence in many parts of the world today. In Sri Lanka, Hindus and Buddhists sometimes violently attack Christians. In Iraq, Shiites and Sunnis kill each other, and the violence between Jews and Palestinians is well known. And this only touches the surface!

Study 2. Proclaiming God's Promises. Acts 13:13-52.
Purpose: To observe Paul's practice of speaking about Jesus first to the Jews in local synagogues and to the God-fearing Gentiles present. This pattern clearly establishes the fact that the gospel is for everyone, and the church is comprised of both Jews and Gentiles.

Question 1. Jews gathered every sabbath in the synagogues to read the Old Testament Scriptures and to worship God. Because the Jews were God's chosen people, who believed in the coming of the Messiah, Paul felt compelled to go to them first with the good news about Jesus (see Acts 13:46). But God-fearing Gentiles also attended synagogue services, and so Paul was able to make contact with both Jews and Gentiles during his initial visit to a city.

Question 2. In Paul's mind, he was not proclaiming a new religion but rather the culmination and fulfillment of God's promises to Israel—especially the promise of a Messiah. Because the Jews knew the story of Israel's history and believed in the messianic promise, Paul tells his audience how Jesus fulfills Jewish expectations.

Question 3. Paul focuses primarily on the fact that Jesus is the fulfillment of Old Testament promises. In verse 23 Paul reminds his hearers of God's covenant promises to David in 2 Samuel 7, which culminate with such statements as "I will establish the throne of his kingdom forever" (v. 13) and "Your house and your kingdom will endure forever before me; your throne will be established forever" (v. 16). Jews understood that these verses would find ultimate fulfillment in the Messiah, who would be a descendant of David. Paul also refers to Psalm 2:7 (v. 33), Isaiah 55:3 (v. 34), Psalm 16:10 (v. 35) and Habakkuk 1:5 (v. 41).

Unlike the Jews of Paul's day, people in our culture are often biblically illiterate and therefore unaware of what the Bible says in both the Old and New Testaments. In some cases, however, unbelievers might be surprised to see how clearly Jesus fulfills certain Old Testament prophecies, such as Isaiah 53. They do not need to share your belief in the divine inspiration of the Bible to appreciate the amazing ways that Jesus fulfills what was said about him in the Old Testament.

Question 4. In both the books of Galatians and Romans Paul demonstrates that keeping the law—whether the law of Moses or the "law" of conscience—could never bring about justification. (The word *justified* comes from the legal system and refers to the judge declaring both the innocence and righteousness of a person in a court of law.) Instead, the law brought only condemnation because people everywhere fall short of God's just requirements (see Rom 1:16–3:20).

Question 6. Jealousy was an odd response. Did they feel that their status and authority as teachers of the law were being threatened by Paul and Barnabas? Were they jealous because the entire city showed up to hear Paul's message, while they had been able to reach only the Jews and some God-fearing Gentiles?

The hostility of the Jews is easier to understand. Not only did they feel their authority and prestige were being threatened, but they also thought Paul and Barnabas were presenting teachings that were contrary to the Old Testament. We should also remember that Gentiles were viewed by Jews as "unclean" and therefore unfit for a relationship with God. Paul was therefore crossing both ethnic and religious lines that were viewed as inviolable in his day.

Study 3. Poor Yet Rich. 1 Corinthians 4:8-13; 2 Corinthians 6:3-10.
Purpose: To grasp the fact that we are rich in Christ regardless of how much money or power or prestige we have in this present age.
Question 3. Paul does not scold the Corinthians because they have these things but because they assume that they are rich and glorious when in fact they are spiritually immature and boastful.
Questions 4-5. Many Christians would feel completely abandoned by God if he allowed such things to happen to them. Those types of hardships would cause them to question God's goodness and love.

Why would they respond that way, especially when God has repeatedly told us that we will experience suffering in this present age (Jn 16:33; Rom 8:17-25; 2 Cor 4:7-15)? Perhaps it is because many evangelicals have wedded Christianity and the American dream. We assume that God owes us a good-paying job, an upwardly mobile career, a loving spouse, two or three children, a house in the suburbs and a trouble-free life. Instead of questioning God's goodness when our dreams fail to materialize, what we need is to rethink our view of life during this present age. We also need to realize the true wealth we do possess in Christ.
Question 7. Paul knows that what is visible to the world—his poverty and suffering—does not reveal the full reality of his life. Even though he is unknown by the world, he is known and loved by God. Even though he is sorrowful because of his sufferings, he has many reasons to rejoice in Christ. Even though he is poor by the world's standards, he possesses untold riches in Christ. Even though his ministry exposes him to a living death, he possesses eternal life and the promise of resurrection. His healthy view of God and himself resulted from seeing the unseen through the eyes of faith.

Study 4. The Power of Praise. Acts 16:16-40.
Purpose: To demonstrate the power of praise and the liberating effects of the gospel.

Introduction. The fourth verse of "And Can It Be That I Should Gain?" has especially strong parallels to Paul and Silas's experience in Acts 16:

Long my imprisoned spirit lay,
Fast bound in sin and nature's night;
Thine eye diffused a quickening ray—
I woke, the dungeon flamed with light;
My chains fell off, my heart was free,
I rose, went forth, and followed Thee.
My chains fell off, my heart was free,
I rose, went forth, and followed Thee.

Question 2. Undoubtedly, Paul was not troubled by the girl's message, which was true, but rather by the fact that she was possessed by an evil spirit (vv. 16, 18). Demon possession was common in Paul's day, and Jesus and the apostles cast out many demons from people during their ministry.

Question 4. After Saul's conversion, the Lord told Ananias that he would show Paul "how much he must suffer for my name" (Acts 9:16). The apostles and early believers—including the martyrs in the early centuries of the church—rejoiced "because they had been counted worthy of suffering disgrace for the Name [of Jesus]" (Acts 5:41). Paul and Silas also trusted in the sovereignty of God and believed that he would deliver them so that they could continue to fulfill their God-given mission (see Phil 1:19-26 for an example of Paul's attitude).

Question 8. Paul's and Silas's rights as Roman citizens had been violated because they had been beaten and thrown into prison without a trial, which was required by Roman law. Paul knew that the law could be used to his advantage to protect him as he went throughout the Empire proclaiming the gospel, so he wasn't about to let the Philippians ignore his rights.

Question 9. Paul reminds us in 2 Timothy 3:12 that "everyone who wants to live a godly life in Christ Jesus will be persecuted." When we look at the book of Acts, we discover that believers were almost never persecuted for being kind and loving to their non-Christian neighbors but rather for the godly practice of proclaiming that belief in Jesus Christ is the only way to receive God's forgiveness and eternal life. If we are not being persecuted in our day, perhaps it is because we are not being faithful in sharing the good news about Jesus with those around us.

People today are increasingly hostile to the idea that Jesus is the only way to God. Even many Christians are offended by it and therefore have embraced the idea that the cross is necessary for salvation and forgiveness but not the gospel. In other words, people can be saved by Jesus Christ without hearing or knowing anything about him or the life-saving message of the gospel. However, the pattern of the New Testament is clear. The apostles and early church members believed that the cross and the gospel are inseparable, and therefore people need to hear the good news about Jesus to be saved. That is why they were willing to suffer hardship, persecution, imprisonment, stoning and even death in order to get the gospel message to a lost world.

Study 5. Becoming a Spiritual Mentor. Acts 20:13-38.
Purpose: To learn from the apostle Paul what it means to be a spiritual mentor.
Question 2. The focus of Paul's teaching was the good news about Jesus Christ and the fact that both Jews and Gentiles must repent and have faith in Jesus (v. 21). Beyond that, Paul also preached whatever else he believed was helpful to the Ephesians (v. 20). The letter to the Ephesians would be the best example of Paul's teaching.
Question 3. Jesus himself had taught, "If anyone would come after me, he must deny himself and take up his cross and follow me. For whoever wants to save his life will lose it, but whoever loses his life for me and for the gospel will save it" (Mk 8:34-35). Paul was the living embodiment of these words and therefore cared nothing about his own life; he only cared about Jesus and the gospel.
Question 5. "The 'elders' (v. 17) were called 'overseers' and told to pastor ('shepherd') the flock—demonstrating that the same men could be called 'elders,' 'overseers' or 'pastors'" (*NIV Study Bible,* ed. Kenneth Barker [Grand Rapids: Zondervan, 1985], note to Acts 20:28). Paul tells the elders that they are to keep watch over the flock as good shepherds. He again tells them to "be on [their] guard" against false teachers who would come in like savage wolves from the outside and also arise from within the church. Paul's personal example to the Ephesian elders, as well as his words of encouragement and warning, provides an excellent summary of what it means to shepherd a church well.
Question 6. It is common to hear today that Christians should be concerned more with "orthopraxy" (behavior) than "orthodoxy" (doctrine). Paul would be alarmed to hear that one should be considered more important than the other, since they are intimately related.
Question 7. Paul doesn't give us many details about how to discern false teachers, although it is clear that he had fully devoted himself to teaching the Ephesians "the whole will of God" (v. 27) and that false teachers would depart from what Paul had taught. I have found it helpful in my lifetime to distinguish primary teachings of the Christian faith, such as the Trinity, the deity of Christ, the full authority of Scripture, the resurrection, the gospel and the second coming, from secondary teachings, such as the mode of baptism, the various views of the millennium, or the roles of men and women. Godly Christians can and do disagree on secondary issues, and we should show each other humble respect in such matters. But without the primary

teachings of the faith, Christianity would no longer exist, and we should never compromise or abandon these beliefs.

Question 9. Instead of coveting or asking for money from others, Paul worked hard so that he could give money to those in need. Clearly, he expects the same from those who follow Jesus Christ.

Study 6. Truth on Trial. Acts 25:23–26:32.

Purpose: To learn from the example of Paul what it means to "always be prepared to give an answer to everyone who asks you to give the reason for the hope that you have" (1 Pet 3:15).

Question 1. John Polhill writes: "Festus's remarks provide nothing new to the narrative, involving only matters that have already surfaced in Acts. That Luke took the time and space to repeat them shows the importance he attached to them. Festus's introduction provides a useful summary for understanding Paul's whole experience. For Festus himself it all began with a petition from the Jews seeking Paul's condemnation (cf. 25:2, 7, 15). Actually, it all started much earlier—with the Jewish crowd in the temple square screaming that such a man "ought not to live" (cf. 22:22). Festus then explained to his important guests in the audience chamber the circumstances of Paul's appeal. Here again one finds him absolving himself of responsibility: 'I found he had done nothing deserving death, but . . . he made his appeal to the Emperor.' Festus seemed to imply that Paul was himself responsible for the whole situation with the unnecessary appeal, as if he had not himself virtually forced Paul to do so because of his own yielding to Jewish pressure. In any event, Festus at least once again acknowledged Paul's innocence (cf. 18f.)" (John B. Polhill, *Acts,* electronic ed., New American Commentary [Nashville: Broadman & Holman, 2001], 26:496).

Question 2. Paul's speech once again follows the standard pattern of defense speeches of the first century. It starts with the *exordium* (introductory address to the king [26:2-3]), proceeds to the *narratio* (the narration of events [26:4-18]) and ends with the *argumentio* (the proof of his case [26:19-23]). Paul acknowledges the acquaintance of the young king with "Jewish customs and controversies," thus implying his suitability to hear his "defense" (26:2-3). Technically this was not a legal defense, but the word is used in a general sense here. For more on Paul's speech and first-century legal defenses see Ajith Fernando, "Paul's Speech Before Agrippa (25:23–26:23)," in *Acts*, NIV Application Commentary Series (Grand Rapids: Zondervan, 1998), p. 594.

Question 4. On the one hand, Paul's speech shows that he understands why devout Jews would oppose his conversion to Christ, since the Christian faith appeared to be not only contrary to Judaism but also the equivalent of blasphemy ("Jesus is Lord"). Paul also powerfully demonstrates why his conversion had to be miraculous, given his former hatred of Jesus and this seemingly new faith.

Question 8. The Bible clearly teaches that people's primary problem with believing in Christ is not intellectual but spiritual. Paul tells us in Romans that although everyone knows the truth about God through creation, they "suppress" that truth and exchange it for a lie, preferring to worship idols of their own making (Rom 1:18-32). Therefore, we must rely on the Spirit of God in conjunction with the proclamation of the gospel to overcome the hardness of people's hearts.

Question 9. Many Christians today find it awkward and uncomfortable presenting the gospel to their family and friends. And it's easy for us to ridicule those who seem to go overboard in their zeal for evangelism. But D. L. Moody once responded to such a critic by saying, "I prefer my method of preaching the gospel more than your method of not preaching it."

Question 10. The book of Acts describes how the gospel spread from Jerusalem to Judea and Samaria and to the ends of the earth in partial fulfillment of Acts 1:8. Through God's sovereignty and Paul's passion, the gospel reaches Rome, the gateway to the rest of the world, by the end of Acts.

Study 7. Strength in Weakness. 2 Corinthians 12:1-10.
Purpose: To discover that God's grace is sufficient for every situation, and to realize that God's power is best displayed in those who are humble and weak, not in those who are strong and proud.

Question 1. Paul was caught up into the "third heaven" (v. 2), which is synonymous with "paradise" (v. 4). (The first heaven is the earth's atmosphere; the second heaven is the realm of the stars and planets.) Paul is not sure whether his remarkable experience took place in his body or out of the body—and he doesn't seem to care (vv. 2-3).

Question 2. Paul apparently was not permitted to describe the details of his vision (v. 4). Yet the sketchy nature of verses 1-4 goes beyond God's prohibition. Paul tells us in verse 6 that he refrains from boasting "so no one will think more of me than is warranted by what I do or say." In other words, Paul wanted people to evaluate him on the basis of his everyday words and actions rather than by a list of impressive credentials (a principle we certainly could use today!).

Some have suggested that Paul is describing some other person rather than himself ("I will boast about a man like that," v. 5). Yet in verse 1 Paul claims that he will go on boasting, describing visions and revelations of the Lord. He would have nothing further to boast about if the experience he recalls happened to someone else. Furthermore, in verse 7 Paul mentions that he was given a thorn in his flesh "to keep me from becoming conceited because of these surpassingly great revelations." That statement would make no sense unless the "great revelations" were Paul's own.

Question 4. Paul's experiences were so incredible, so extraordinary, that he struggled with pride. As an apostle, he knew he was a member of Christ's most elite corps. And his spiritual experiences were so spectacular that even the other apostles, not to mention "ordinary Christians," were tempted to envy him. But before he had a chance to become conceited, to soar aloft with feelings of superiority, God nailed his feet to earth: "To keep me from becoming conceited because of these surpassingly great revelations, there was given me a thorn in my flesh, a messenger of Satan, to torment me" (v. 7).

For centuries people have speculated about the precise nature of Paul's thorn. They have suggested it was headaches, earaches, eye disease or malarial fever. Others have claimed it was epilepsy, a speech impediment, hypochondria, deafness or remorse for persecuting Christians. Still others have suggested gallstones, gout, rheumatism, a dental infection—even lice! Whatever it was, Paul didn't like it. "Three times I pleaded with the Lord to take it away from me" (v. 8). The thorn not only kept Paul humble, it tormented him and made him feel weak. So he prayed and prayed for its removal.

Question 5. God's answer surprised Paul: "But he said to me, 'My grace is sufficient for you, for my power is made perfect in weakness'" (v. 9). Instead of removing Paul's thorn, God gave him the grace to endure it. Instead of taking away Paul's weakness, God used it to demonstrate his power. The same principle applies to us. Notice that the Lord did not say, "My power is made perfect in your thorn," but rather, "My power is made perfect in weakness" (v. 9). God's promise applies to anything that makes us feel weak, humble and dependent on God.

Questions 6-7. Paul mentions weaknesses, insults, hardships, persecutions and difficulties (v. 10). None of the items in Paul's list is exactly the same as his thorn. But because they shared certain points of similarity with the consequences of his thorn, Paul knew God's grace was sufficient for them all. The same is true today. We probably don't suffer from the same kind of thorn Paul did. But we too face weaknesses, insults, hardships, persecutions and difficulties—things that humble us and make us dependent on God. Whatever the nature of our thorn, like Paul we can confidently rely on Christ's grace and power.

Study 8. Feeling Safe in a Storm. Acts 27:1-44.
Purpose: To learn from Paul's example how to trust God in the midst of life's storms.
Introduction. Samuel Kelly is quoted in Richard Russell Lawrence, *The Mammoth Book of Storms, Shipwrecks and Sea Disasters* (New York: Carroll

& Graf, 2004), p. 1. The "typical merchant ship" information is from Robert H. Gundry, *A Survey of the New Testament* (Grand Rapids: Zondervan, 2003), p. 28.

Question 1. Notice especially how the narrative suddenly shifts in verse 1 to "we," as Luke alerts his readers that he accompanied Paul on this voyage.

Question 2. "Subsequent events proved that Paul's advice was sound: they should have remained at Fair Havens. The season for sea travel was coming to a close. 'The fast' (v. 9) refers to the Day of Atonement. Calculated by the phases of the moon, the Day of Atonement fell at various times from year to year but always in late September or early October. For ancient travel on the Mediterranean, mid-September to early November was considered a dangerous time for traveling the open sea. After early November such travel ceased altogether and generally was not resumed until the beginning of February at the earliest. Paul's advice was based on this well-known fact. It was well into the dangerous season. Any travel now would be risky business" (John B. Polhill, *Acts,* electronic ed., New American Commentary [Nashville: Broadman & Holman, 2001], 26:518).

Question 5. Kenneth Gangel writes: "Here's the heart of the chapter. . . . We need to see the light of heaven shining on a dark and driven ship and on its lost and lonely passengers. Paul already knew he would make it through (23:11). Like Abraham interceding for Sodom, Paul likely pleaded with God to save the lives of his traveling companions. Now, presumably in response to his prayers for his traveling companions, he reports the angel's message: **God has graciously given you the lives of all who sail with you.**

"Doubtless many gods had received repeated appeals during that two weeks; in a situation like this, the most calloused pagan can all of a sudden find words addressed to some kind of deity who might intervene in a time of obvious disaster. Only one God answered! The angelic messenger was quite precise—they would not only be saved, but the ship would **run aground on some island.** . . . Luke records no response to Paul's promise. Had the men cheered or fallen on their knees on the deck to worship Paul's God, we can be sure Luke would have told us. Instead, they would wait to see whether this promise of hope had any substance" (Kenneth O. Gangel, *Acts,* Holman New Testament Commentary [Nashville: Broadman & Holman, 1998], 5:450, bold in original).

Question 7. Luke feels free to express two perspectives that seem to be in tension in this passage: (1) God's sovereign promise and (2) the responsibility of those who heard the promise. Our understanding of the Bible suffers when we try to resolve such tensions in a way that makes sense to us but ends up ignoring part of what Scripture has affirmed. It is beyond our capacity to understand how God's sovereignty and human responsibility can both be true, but consistently the Bible affirms each side of the equation.

Study 9. Finding Hope in God's Kingdom. Acts 28:11-31.
Purpose: To see why the gospel that is offensive to some provides great hope to those who believe.

Question 2. Although Paul is still a prisoner, it is clear that the experiences aboard ship had a powerful effect on the soldiers, so that they allow him a considerable amount of freedom during the final leg of their journey to Rome.

Question 3. The *NIV Study Bible* states that Paul "had committed no flagrant crime and was not a politically dangerous rival. So he was allowed to have his own living quarters, but a guard was with him at all times, perhaps chained to him" (*NIV Study Bible,* ed. Kenneth Barker [Grand Rapids: Zondervan, 1985], note to Acts 28:16).

Question 4. "It was, then, to inform the Roman Jews accurately about the situation that Paul had called them together. For in fact what was at issue in his trial, as he had insisted all along, was the true nature of *the hope of Israel* in the coming of the Messiah and the resurrection. It was, in other words, for being a loyal Jew, as he saw it, that Paul was wearing a Roman fetter, and this was surely something that demanded the attention of the Jews, since their religion was legally permitted by the Romans" (I. Howard Marshall, *Acts,* Tyndale New Testament Commentaries [Downers Grove, Ill.: InterVarsity Press, 1988], p. 423).

Question 5. If any group in Paul's day had sincere faith in God it would have been the Jews. They studied the Scriptures, believed in Yahweh and sought diligently to follow the Mosiac law. Paul tells us in Romans 10:2, "I can testify about them that they are zealous for God." Yet in spite of their many privileges, Paul still says, "Brothers, my heart's desire and prayer to God for the Israelites is that they may be saved. . . . Their zeal is not based on knowledge. Since they did not know the righteousness that comes from God and sought to establish their own, they did not submit to God's righteousness. Christ is the end of the law so that there may be righteousness for everyone who believes" (Rom 10:1-4). Paul realized that the Jewish people still needed to be saved because they had not submitted to God's righteousness provided freely in Christ and because they had not believed in the true Messiah.

Questions 7-8. Isaiah contrasts the differences between hearing versus understanding and seeing versus perceiving. The difference in both cases is that the message has not penetrated the heart, which has become calloused. Whenever we hear or read the Scriptures, we need to guard the condition of our hearts by responding to the message with both faith and obedience.

Question 10. Many Christians, especially in the West, focus almost exclusively on personal salvation through Jesus Christ and fail to grasp that his salvation will eventually encompass the whole of creation. That all-encompassing work of Christ is known throughout the Bible as the kingdom of God.

Study 10. Experiencing Joy in Sufferings. Philippians 1:12-26.

Purpose: To look at the secret to true joy and happiness as seen through the eyes of the apostle Paul.

Introduction. Story taken from Edmund Morris, *The Rise of Theodore Roosevelt* (New York: Coward, McCann & Geoghegan, 1979), pp. 212-20.

Question 2. People often claim that Paul is able to be joyful in prison because joy is different from happiness. Supposedly, happiness is dependent on personal circumstances, while joy is not. Yet in this passage, Paul's joy is dependent on his circumstances—although not those related to his personal comfort. He clearly states in verses 12 and following that his circumstances have "served to advance the gospel." Paul is able to be joyful in prison because he values the preaching of the gospel more than he does his own comfort and freedom.

Question 4. Paul's greatest value in life was Jesus Christ. He ordered his priorities, his goals, his time and all of his energy around one central focus—to live for Christ. Many of us pay lip service to that statement, and it may even be partially true for some of us. But if we were to honestly examine our daily lives and what motivates most of our actions, we'd have to reword Philippians 1:21: "For to me, to live is . . . ME!" We tend to value our comfort, our peace, our entertainment and our pleasure. Many of us are not Christ-centered, but self-centered.

Question 5. "Verse 23 specifies that the gain brought by death is 'being with Christ,' so that here Paul is saying that his ultimate concern and most precious possession, both now and forever, is Christ and his relationship to him" (*NIV Study Bible*, ed. Kenneth Barker [Grand Rapids: Zondervan, 1985], note to Phil 1:21).

Question 7. Paul knows that there can be only two outcomes to his imprisonment: freedom or death. And of those two alternatives, he would prefer to die and be with his Savior and Lord, Jesus Christ. Even though Paul does not know for certain what the outcome will be, he is convinced that the Philippians still need his help for their "progress and joy in the faith," and therefore he is convinced that the Lord will arrange for him to be set free to serve them. Because Paul lives for Christ, he is again willing to set aside his personal preferences for the sake of the gospel and the Christians at Philippi.

Jack Kuhatschek is executive vice president and publisher at Baker Publishing Group and the author of many Bible study guides, including Galatians *and* Romans *in the LifeGuide® Bible Study series, and the books* Applying the Bible *and* The Superman Syndrome.

What Should We Study Next?

A good place to continue your study of Scripture would be with a book study. Many groups begin with a Gospel such as *Mark* (20 studies by James Hoover) or *John* (26 studies by Douglas Connelly). These guides are divided into two parts so that if twenty or twenty-six weeks seems like too much to do at once, the group can feel free to do half and take a break with another topic. Later you might want to come back to it. You might prefer to try a shorter letter. *Philippians* (9 studies by Donald Baker), *Ephesians* (11 studies by Andrew T. and Phyllis J. Le Peau) and *1 & 2 Timothy and Titus* (11 studies by Pete Sommer) are good options. If you want to vary your reading with an Old Testament book, consider *Ecclesiastes* (12 studies by Bill and Teresa Syrios) for a challenging and exciting study.

There are a number of interesting topical LifeGuide studies as well. Here are some options for filling three or four quarters of a year:

Basic Discipleship
Christian Beliefs, 12 studies by Stephen D. Eyre
Christian Character, 12 studies by Andrea Sterk & Peter Scazzero
Christian Disciplines, 12 studies by Andrea Sterk & Peter Scazzero
Evangelism, 12 studies by Rebecca Manley Pippert & Ruth Siemens

Building Community
Fruit of the Spirit, 9 studies by Hazel Offner
Spiritual Gifts, 8 studies by R. Paul Stevens
Christian Community, 10 studies by Rob Suggs

Character Studies
David, 12 studies by Jack Kuhatschek
New Testament Characters, 10 studies by Carolyn Nystrom
Old Testament Characters, 12 studies by Peter Scazzero
Women of the Old Testament, 12 studies by Gladys Hunt

The Trinity
Meeting God, 12 studies by J. I. Packer
Meeting Jesus, 13 studies by Leighton Ford
Meeting the Spirit, 10 studies by Douglas Connelly